漢達的驚奇

HANDA'S SURPRISE

Eileen Browne

Chinese translation by Sylvia Denham

mantra

漢達將七個美味的水果放入籃裏，準備拿去給她的朋友雅姬。

Handa put seven delicious fruits in a basket for her friend, Akeyo.

漢達出發往雅姬的村落時，她估計雅姬必定會感到驚喜。

She will be surprised, thought Handa as she set off for Akeyo's village.

不知她最喜歡那一種水果呢？

I wonder which fruit she'll like best?

她會喜歡又軟又黃的香蕉⋯

Will she like the soft yellow banana ...

抑或是又香又甜的番石榴呢？

or the sweet-smelling guava?

她會喜歡又圓又多汁的橙⋯

Will she like the round juicy orange ...

抑或是又熟又紅的芒果呢？

or the ripe red mango?

她會喜歡有尖葉的菠蘿⋯

Will she like the spiky-leaved pineapple ...

抑或是奶油綠色的牛油果…

the creamy green avocado ...

還是又濃又紫的番蓮果呢?

or the tangy purple passion-fruit?

Which fruit will Akeyo like best?

究竟雅姬會喜歡那一種呢？

"Hello, Akeyo," said Handa. "I've brought you a surprise."

「你好！雅姬，」漢達説，「我爲你帶來驚喜呀。」

「柑桔！」雅姬說，「我最喜歡的水果。」
「柑桔？」漢達說，「那眞是意想不到！」

"Tangerines!" said Akeyo. "My favourite fruit."
"TANGERINES?" said Handa. "That *is* a surprise!"

monkey

ostrich

zebra

elephant

giraffe

antelope

parrot

goat